Writing

historical

fiction

viewing the past through the lens of the present

✳ Writing Lessons from the Front

book
8

DR. ANGELA HUNT

ANGELA HUNT

Other Books in the Writing Lessons from the Front Series

The Plot Skeleton, Book 1

Creating Extraordinary Characters, Book 2

Point of View, Book 3

Track Down the Weasel Words, Book 4

Evoking Emotion, Book 5

Plans and Processes, Book 6

Tension on the Line, Book 7

Writing Historical Fiction, Book 8

A Christian Writer's Possibly Useful Ruminations on a Life in Pages,
supplemental volume

Hunt Haven

Visit Angela Hunt's Web site at www.angelahuntbooks.com

ISBN: 0692220097
ISBN-13: 978-0692220092

ii

In memory of Katherine Hulme and
Marie Louise Habets—whose story taught me to savor times
and places far beyond my ken.

THE ONE AND ONLY CHAPTER

I've always loved historical fiction. While I was still in elementary school I discovered a box of old abandoned books in our rental house, and I loved those books so much I carried them with me when my husband and I moved into a house of our own. Inside the corrugated walls of that box I found copies of *Jane Eyre*, *The Nun's Story*, and *Gone with the Wind* . . . and in reading those historical novels, I fell in love with other worlds and other eras.

I still have a couple of those books, and I've read them many times over the years. That's a beautiful thing about historical fiction—it's timeless.

I don't know if an "official" definition exists for this genre, but you might say that historical fiction *is a novel set during a distinct period in history.* This time period might or might not be before the author's time. For instance, *The Nun's Story*, set in the years of World War II, wasn't considered historical fiction when it was published in 1956, but it qualifies today. I wouldn't apply a historical fiction label to *The Pearl*, my 2003 novel about cloning, but my grandchildren might.

Historical fiction is a broad genre encompassing a host of subgenres: romance, thrillers, the "history mystery," biblical novels, fantasy, "alternative history" (e.g. what if the Confederacy had won the Civil War?), science fiction, westerns, time travel, and many more. If you can imagine a story set in the past, you can research the setting for a historical novel and write it for juveniles or adults.

Who reads historical novels? Lots of people, but not everyone. I have observed a certain prejudice against historical novels among some readers, particularly if the novels seem daunting in plot, "history lessons," or language ("too many thee's and thou's," reported one reader). I am personally chagrinned whenever I open a book and find a chart of the protagonist's extended family on the fourth page. I can't help feeling that if I need a diagram to keep up, how could the book be a relaxing, entertaining read?

But not all historical novels are hard or difficult to read— the best ones are as entertaining as their contemporary versions. And they offer something contemporary novels don't—a detailed look into a world gone by, an age when people much like ourselves lived and loved and struggled against overwhelming odds.

The best historical novels entertain us by providing a cast of memorable, fascinating characters. When we become glued to the story because we can't wait to see what Scarlett or Pip will do next, the historical aspect seems almost incidental.

For most readers, historical novels offer more than an entertaining story—they also provide the reader with an enjoyable learning experience. As readers travel through the historical story world with the characters, they live through the vicarious experiences of living in another time, eating unusual foods, and observing unusual customs. A skillful historical novelist will populate her novel with lots of sensory details to enliven and enlarge the experience.

When I asked my blog readers to chime in with reasons why they liked to read historical fiction, I received several interesting answers:

From Linda: "I love historical fiction because it fascinates me to learn how people dealt with the challenges of daily life in those times, yet the interpersonal issues are timeless. It's easy to romanticize life 'way back when,' but daily life was hard--and yet people still loved, laughed, cried, hurt. [Historical fiction] gives me a greater appreciation for what we have today."

Kara wrote that she and a friend "like historical fiction because the time period is different than today. We live life today; we know what it's like. Historical fiction transports us to another time where life was not necessarily simpler, but different." She adds that contemporary fiction often "hits too close to home" in its subject matter, but the same subject in historical fiction allows for a certain emotional distance.

Holly likes historical fiction because "I learn about how people lived during various times in history--from traveling across the country in a wagon to sailing across the sea to life in communist Russia (all things I have never experienced). It teaches me something new. Also, I am transported to view another place and time, which thrills me!"

Margaret wrote that she enjoys historical fiction "because it is about events that really happened. Since those things occurred in the past, we can trace the outcome of those events. When we gain a deeper understanding of the beliefs and motivations of people in history and how these played out in the results of their actions, we gain important insights that help us make better decisions in the present."

Indeed. As George Santayana said, "Those who cannot remember the past are condemned to repeat it."

Pick a Time, Any Time!

What time periods are open to an author considering historical fiction? Nearly all of them! No period of time is too early to explore. Jean Auel's prehistoric novels are best-sellers. Tosca Lee's novel, *Havah*, is about Eve, the first woman on the planet.

Some historical periods have been explored more than others (the Civil War comes to mind), so the writer considering one of these eras had better come up with a unique twist on her story. You're more likely to pique an editor's interest if you're writing in a time period that hasn't been over-represented in your chosen market. So visit your local bookstore, make a note of what's on the shelves, and then *choose something else*. Why set out to be similar when you could be strikingly original?

Notice that I said *nearly* all time periods are open to the historical novelist. You can go back as far as you like, but be careful when considering more recent history. When I started writing, World War II books weren't considered historical, but now they are. The boundary line is always shifting, so if you want to write a book set in the disco world of the 1980s, better check with an editor to see if your book would be considered historical. Here's a tip—if you know lots of people who lived through the period you're considering, it's probably not unfamiliar enough to be deemed "historical."

Historical Settings

Where should you set your historical novel? The answer depends on the size of your story canvas. Is your story broad, with a cast of many characters and involving incidents of war, disease, or major national calamity? Then set your story in the midst of the action and feature the people who faced the most significant changes. For instance, if you want to write a heroic adventure novel focused on the 1986 Challenger explosion, you should set it at Cape Kennedy or Houston.

But if your story is smaller, if you plan on writing about the effects of the Challenger disaster on an astronaut's estranged wife, then you could set it in a small town in Alabama, where the woman hears about her husband's death and wonders why the people around her continue with life-as-usual while for her time is standing still.

Wherever you set your novel, remember that for the story to be effective, you must shrink any major event down to a size that will greatly affect your protagonist. "When writing about war," the old writing adage goes, "write about one man's war."

On September 11, 2001, I was in Springfield, Missouri, with my friend Lori Copeland. We had just finished writing one of our Heavenly Daze novels, and that morning I was getting ready to go to the airport. I had the television on, and watched as a second jet tore through the second tower at the World Trade Center.

I called upstairs to Lori and her husband, and together we huddled before the television and watched the horrific events unfold. We saw the disasters at the Pentagon and in

Pennsylvania; we stared as the New York towers crumbled to the ground and dust-coated people ran screaming through the streets. As I watched, the writer part of my brain kept thinking, *How could I write about this? I can't. It's too big. Too horrible. Too big.*

Many novelists, of course, have written stories about what happened on that terrible September 11th, but each of them narrowed the spotlight until it shone only on one or two people. My book club recently read *Extremely Loud and Incredibly Close*, by Jonathan Safran Foer, and I was impressed at how skillfully the author wrapped that huge event around a young autistic boy who lost his father when the towers fell.

So if you want to write about the Vietnam War, the fall of Jericho, the exodus from Egypt, or the first moon landing, wrap your world event around one extremely interesting protagonist. Let us experience the events of that time through his or her eyes, and your reader will experience the situation for himself. Take the event that is "too big" to handle, and shrink it to a mallet that smacks your protagonist's ordinary world and sends it spinning out of control.

Now you're ready to proceed.

Wait—what about your plot? Don't you need a plot before you begin researching?

Not necessarily. You may have a vague idea about your story's focus and direction, but keep an open mind as you dig into the research. You may discover little nuggets of information that will greatly enrich your plot and add key complications to your story.

When I set out to write my first adult novel, I talked with the editor for whom I'd written several juvenile novels. He'd asked me to consider adult fiction, and I was happy to expand my horizons. Our conversation went something like this:

"So," I began, "what would you like me to submit? A contemporary novel or historical?"

"Historicals seem to be selling best right now."

"Okay. What about the time period? Any preference?"

"The Civil War has been done to death . . . and so has life

9

on the prairie."

"Okay . . . hmm. I can't think of any Christian novels set in medieval times. What about that era?"

"Go for it."

And so I did.

I went to my office and began to research medieval times—and I learned that those years were called the Dark Ages for good reason. Most people were illiterate, the Catholic church was the only established church in Europe, and people tended to be either very wealthy or very poor.

I sketched out a plot about the beautiful daughter of a poor villein (the English version of a serf) who grows up in a castle as a playmate to the nobleman's daughter. When the noble family has no more use for her—especially when it becomes clear that she has fallen in love with the nobleman's oldest son—they marry her off to the village brute.

My poor protagonist would be abused and unloved, but she would conquer her foes and find true love and happiness at the end of the story.

But . . . what about the middle of the book? What sorts of complications could I create that would forge a will of iron in my gentle protagonist?

As I researched medieval society and common beliefs of the period, I learned that during the Middle Ages people believed that twins were the result of a woman's union with two different men. Ah! Perfect.

My protagonist's brutish husband had been cruel enough, but after giving birth to one child, when she shrieks and prepares to give birth to yet another, the man flies into a rage and is determined to kill her for her adultery.

Research provided a perfectly logical and fascinating development to move my story forward and turn my gentle heroine into a steely-eyed woman bent on revenge.

First, We Create Characters

In *Creating Extraordinary Characters*, the second lesson in the Writing Lessons series, I give tips on how to create characters that are larger than life. Those lessons still apply when you're writing historical fiction, because without characters, plot is just stage direction.

If your characters seem a bit blank when you're just starting out, don't worry. As you research and fine-tune your plot, you'll begin to understand what your characters must be in order to carry off the story. I never feel that I know my characters until I've finished the first draft. We're like strangers mingling at a party, sharing a few whispers and hinting at buried secrets. By the time I finish the second or third draft, however, I could tell you what my characters like to eat for dinner.

Here's a useful tip on naming historical characters. If you're writing an American character who was born sometime after 1880, be sure to visit Social Security's baby name   database: http://www.ssa.gov/oact/babynames/decades/

This site lists the most popular 100 baby names by year and decade, and even though "John" and "Mary" ruled the lists for years, you can find some memorable and appropriate-for-the-time names in those long lists.

If you're naming characters who lived well before the nineteenth century, skim through the original sources you've used for research. The people mentioned within those pages are likely to have names common to the time.

I also heartily recommend Writer's Digest's *Character Naming Sourcebook* by Sherrilyn Kenyon.[1] Along with several interesting articles about the importance of character names, this book offers lists of names grouped by geographic and/or historical categories. So you can find names for your Arthurian knight, your Greek fisherman, your Native American trapper (listed by tribe!), and your Welsh poet. A wonderful tool now available in print and e-book editions.

Next, We Research

No matter when or where you set your historical novel, you should pay attention to a key convention of the genre: get your history right. Though some authors do exercise artistic license and take liberties with recorded history, I'd advise against it. Unless you're writing a novel of alternative history ("Imagine a world in which Hitler completely conquered Europe"), historical readers want to trust that you've done your homework.

We've all seen notes from the author at the back of a novel explaining why he moved the Battle of Shewbury from Monday to Thursday. If you absolutely *have* to change recorded history, be sure to mention it in an afterword or other commentary. If you don't, some sharp-eyed historian will take you to task in an email, write a horrible review on Amazon.com, and generally let it be known that you are a novelist who does not research properly.

(Sometimes they do those things even if you *do* research properly. If your version contradicts the sappy Hollywood version of an historic event, you will be branded as a heretic even though you are correct and Hollywood is wrong. That's when you take a deep breath and repeat: "Life is too short to waste time with critics.")

For years now, I have listed my sources and references in the back of my historical novels. First, I think it's fair and a nice gesture to acknowledge the authors whose work helped me write a story. Second, it's a subtle way to show the reader that you have done your homework. Finally, some readers become fascinated with a story or historical era, and a list of references sends them off to learn more about your chosen time period.

A bibliographic list is certainly not a necessity, but I think the advantages of including such a list far outweigh the option of not including one.

Though I could spend an entire day exploring rabbit trails, I force myself to remember that the first phase of research is the Macro Phase. I need to learn about "big picture" concepts and issues; I do not yet need to learn about trivial details.

So here's a checklist of general areas we need to research

as we begin our novels:

____Society: What were the prevailing attitudes of society? How did society treat men, women, children, and slaves? Were most people educated and if so, how? What were the jobs of ordinary people? What were the prevailing attitudes toward racial differences?

____Housing: Where did most people live? How were homes constructed? How did the homes of the wealthy differ from those of the poor? Did wealthy and poor neighbors ever mix? Did they ever intermarry?

____Religion: What was the prevailing religion, and how did it influence the common man's daily life? Who were the religious authorities of that time and place? What sort of power did they have—ecclesiastical or governmental or both? What sort of religious education did the common man receive, and how did he receive it? What did the Church, temple, or sacred place mean to him? Was his relationship with his god personal or prescribed?
Incidentally, I've had occasional Amazon reviewers chide me for "inserting" my "Christian beliefs" into a historical story when all I did was paint a realistic picture of an era in which evangelism and the Christian religion were high priorities. Unfortunately, the average modern reader has no idea that the practice of religion and discussion of religious topics was woven into the fabric of historical cultures and societies. Frankly, I would be suspicious if I read a historical novel in which characters did not place a high value on religion and man's relationship with God. Secularism did not begin to pervade Western society until after the nineteenth century rise of Darwinism.

____Government: Who was king or prime minister or president in your protagonist's nation? What sort of government was in place, and how did its work, taxes, and wars affect the people of your story? Did governmental authorities keep their distance, or did they meddle in the daily lives of your characters?

____Daily life: What did your characters eat and how did they obtain their food? How was food preserved, served, and obtained? How much time was spent in the preparing and storage of food? Was the food supply seasonal? If so, how did the seasons of scarcity and plenty affect your characters?

How did the common man travel from place to place? How would your protagonist transport goods? (A great many Christmas movies and nativity stories were ruined for me when I researched the novella, *The Nativity Story*. I learned that donkeys were used to carry water jars, bedding, and supplies when people traveled from one city to another. So Mary probably didn't ride that donkey on her journey to Bethlehem, she walked. Which makes me respect her all the more.)

____ What language(s) did your protagonist speak? What sort of music could he hear, and when did he hear it? What did your characters do for recreation?

____Clothing: what did people wear to work? To church? How did garments for the wealthy differ from clothing from the poor? What about underwear? How did mothers dress their children? Did they diaper their babies? How long did it take a woman to get dressed—and would she require help from a servant? How did men wear their hair—and how did it differ from women's hairstyles? What might you find in a typical character's closet or trunk?

I have several books about clothing on my shelf, the most useful of which is *Costume 1066-1966*, by John Peacock (Thames and Hudson, 1986, 2006). I'm sure there are newer versions of books like this, but this one has always given me clothing for men and women by regnal year. It's been invaluable.)

____Weather/climate: How did the weather and climate of your story setting affect your characters? (Florida, for instance, wasn't densely settled until the invention of air conditioning.) How did technology—or the lack of it—shape your story world? How will it affect your characters over the course of the novel? Will the climate and/or setting greatly affect your characters' health?

____Medicine: What illnesses were prevalent during this era? Any prevalent plagues? Did people understand the concept of germs and contamination? How did they dispose of the dead? How did women endure childbirth? How did superstition and/or religion affect medical practice? Who were the medical experts—doctors, witch doctors, or religious leaders? Where did the sick go for treatment? How was surgery, if any, accomplished? What was used to alleviate pain? What was the average lifespan? How high was the infant mortality rate?

____The world: what was known about creation in your story era? About the origin of man? What scientific discoveries were made during this time period? What countries were born, and what kingdoms overthrown? What technology existed as your story begins, and what new technologies could have arrived during the course of your novel?

The questions I've asked are not meant to be exhaustive—in fact, I've only scratched the surface of the overall concepts we need to investigate before beginning a historical novel.

Make the Information Accessible

So . . . how do we conduct all this research? And how do we remember everything we will need to know?

First, we read. Find books on your time period and begin to skim through them, absorbing concepts, big picture ideas, and miscellaneous information. Don't worry about memorizing details, but set up some kind of note taking system so you'll know where to find the details when you need them.

When I first began to write historical novels, I devised a system of notecards. I limited the notecards to one topic each, and I jotted the name of the source in a corner so I could always go directly to the book to read further.

All the note-taking in the world won't help you if you can't find a specific note when you need it. Once I became familiar with computer databases, I did the same thing on "virtual" notecards, jotting down little bits of information on small cards and mentioning the name of the source. I used to use an expensive database called *Ask Sam*, and it was invaluable because I could simply type in a word—"donkey"—and immediately find the book where I'd read that women did not ride donkeys in ancient Palestine.

These days I write in Scrivener[2], an easy to use writing program that lets me keep my research in the same file as my manuscript. My notes are still computer-searchable, so I can find the quote or information I need with a few keystrokes. And now that so much trustworthy information is found online, I can highlight a section of text on a website, click a key, and have it immediately pasted into my research notes. Technology is wonderful . . . when it works.

When the information you need is not on the Internet (or if what's on the Internet isn't trustworthy), buy books and mark useful pages with highlighting and sticky tabs. If your budget doesn't allow you to buy many books, go to the library and make copious notes on note cards or your laptop.

A caveat: read novels set in your chosen time period at your own risk. I never allow myself to trust the accuracy of other novelists, especially since I heard one writer say that if she didn't know something, she simply "made something up!" Even the most careful of writers has to invent *some* facts, and how can a reader know which facts were researched and which were invented?

If you shouldn't rely on novels, what sorts of books should you read for research? Anything and everything else. Children's nonfiction books can be helpful because they tend to boil topics down to the important highlights. Children's paper doll books can give great insight as to the clothing and hairstyles of an era. Textbooks, biographies, and nonfiction books of all types may prove useful.

Once I was browsing in an antique store and spotted an old scrapbook, filled with clippings from nineteenth century newspapers. I quickly paid five dollars to buy the book, then took it home, amazed by the clippings from the Civil War era newspapers. The papers printed detailed obituaries, prayers, religious lessons . . . amazing. You never know what you'll find if you keep your eyes open.

Most useful of all are books written in the era you've chosen for your story. Yes, you can find ancient writings. I used several translated ancient Egyptian texts in my "Joseph" novels, and I used the sixteenth-century diaries of John White to write my novel on the lost colony of Roanoke. Original sources are invaluable to a historical novelist.

Speaking of John White . . . After *Roanoke* was published, someone wrote to my publisher and complained that I had made a mistake in the book because I mentioned idols. She insisted that the original native Americans did not participate in idol worship.

When my publisher quizzed me about it, I flipped through the book and found the disputed paragraph:

> "The Indians are truly capable of Christian love," her uncle had once written her father, "for they naturally share all things in common and know neither jealousy, selfishness, or ambition. They believe that one god created the world, and another restored it after the great flood. They have part of the truth and part of the nature of Christ, but they worship idols, fallen spirits, and can be most cruel to

> their enemies. We have a most urgent
> responsibility to bring them to the truth of the
> Gospel of Jesus Christ."

Once I found and identified the reference to idols, I was happy to report that *I* hadn't said the natives worshipped idols—John White did, for the words I used came directly from one of his letters. Granted, White assumed the Indians' carved images were idols while we would probably call them *totems*. Still, what was a sixteenth-century Englishman to think? Allowing historical characters to speak for themselves is a wonderful way to steep your story in authenticity.

In the macro research phase, you goal is to gather information to help you understand the overall world of your characters. As you begin to ingest this information, you will discover interesting facts that you can use to flesh out your plot ideas. If you discover something surprising, grab onto that nugget and record it where you'll be sure to have access to it. Anything that surprises you will probably surprise your reader as well. And that's a huge part of what makes reading so rewarding and entertaining.

At Some Point, Stop

Someone recently asked me, "Is it possible to research too much?" In a word, yes. Some writers, myself included, suffer from the Fear of the Blank Screen. If you enjoy research (and people who suffer from Blank Screen Phobia find almost *anything* more enjoyable than beginning the dreaded first draft), you can be tempted to research for months when a week would suffice.

Step 2: Sketch Out Your Plot Skeleton

The first Writing Lesson front the Front book, *The Plot Skeleton*, thoroughly discusses how to construct and plan a plot, so I won't rehash that material here. (If you haven't read that book, you probably should. A historical novel does not work without a structurally sound plot.)

Take what you've learned from your research, place your protagonist in your nascent story world, and begin to sketch out scenes that fit your story skeleton. I use notecards, either paper cards or the virtual cards in Scrivener, and on each I simply write a sentence or two about what will happen in each scene:

> This is where Jocelyn goes to dinner with
> the brothers and their mother.

Once you have a stack of scene cards (I tend to divide the plot into thirds and tackle each third separately), you're ready to begin writing your first draft scenes. Remember: the goal of a first draft is not to create something beautiful, **it's to get the story down.**

When you find that you've written

Jocelyn shoved her voluminous skirt aside and sat down to a plate of –

If you have no idea what Jocelyn would be eating at the Duke's palace, insert brackets and something like this:

[find out what's on the menu at Duke's!]

and keep writing.

I'm a *huge* believer in getting the story down before you do any backtracking or editing. Too many writers get sidetracked trying to fill in the blanks, and they never finish that first draft.

Pushing that first draft out is just like birthing a baby. You sweat and groan and find the process a painful ordeal, but when that squalling mess arrives on your desk, you're elated. You can always clean up a mess. Your book exists. You've done it. You've written (the first draft of) a book.

After an hour or a day or a week of celebration, take time for a day of triage—you need to fix the manuscript where it's bleeding. Search for brackets, and when you spot your note about finding out what they were eating at the Duke's, now you have to time to do *micro* research, getting all the details right.

After you've filled in all your bracket queries, go back and make sure you haven't contradicted any recorded history. You'll find it helpful to create a timeline (you can design a simple one in Microsoft Excel), and make sure that the historic Battle of Waterloo, which occurred on Sunday, June 18th, 1815, doesn't occur on Friday in your story. If George met Martha for the first time in Vicksburg, you can't have them meeting in Richmond.

How do you do this? Simple. On the Excel spreadsheet, assign each scene to a row. Use the columns to keep track of whatever information you need—I use Point of View (who is the POV character in each scene), date, time, action, weather, dramatic question raised, dramatic question answered, and anything else I need for the story.

By assigning each scene to a date, I can see where I need to insert phrases like "Four weeks later, George went to Vicksburg . . ." or "Later that afternoon . . ."

Not only do timelines help you keep track of important historical dates, but they help a novelist remember that characters do move through weeks and holidays. Many times I have written about people going to work day after day, but a timeline helped me realize that I forgot to mention weekends. Or I've had women get pregnant and go through December without ever mentioning Christmas—a huge event for every family, every year. Keeping a good timeline will help anchor your novel to the real world, past or present.

When Historical Sources Disagree

What do you do when the historical experts don't agree on times, dates, or places? You're more likely to run into this problem when you write about ancient eras—eighteenth dynasty Egypt, for instance, or almost any period of Old Testament history. In this situation, a novelist is forced to gather as many expert opinions as possible and then make an informed choice. Choose the option that best fits with the other facts you've learned about the period.

And do not be afraid to trust the Bible in its original form (some translations use euphemisms that can lead you astray). Time after time, its veracity has been verified by archeological discoveries. I would trust it above any other source.

Speaking of the Bible—some people assume that "biblical fiction" and "historical fiction about Bible characters" are the same thing, but to me they are quite different. I doubt if many other people share my opinion, but to me the key difference lies in how the book is written.

A novelist may take a Bible story and flesh it out, drawing mostly on religious books and commentaries.

Or a novelist may take biblical characters and flesh them out, drawing on religious books and historical documents and ancient texts.

While both methods are certainly legitimate, I enjoy the latter approach, and in examining other records from the time of biblical characters, I have discovered logical complications and plot developments not even hinted at in the Bible. Because so much of the novel is based on extra-biblical material, I consider it more historical fiction than purely biblical.

In writing historical novels featuring Joseph, Moses, Esther, Mary Magdalene, and the nativity, I've found fascinating facts in Jewish texts, agnostic accounts, and even books written from an Islamic perspective. I don't agree with everything I read, of course, but learning to see historical events from other perspectives helps me sharpen my own.

For instance, as I began to develop my novel on Esther, I knew I had to come up with story elements no one had used before. Nearly everyone—Christians and Jews—knows the story of the brave, beautiful girl who courageously confronted a king and saved her people, so how could I tell the story in a unique way?

In search of an answer, I studied every book I could find on ancient Persia. I studied the government, the historical figures, the architecture, the palaces. I studied biographies of Xerxes, the king; Darius, his father; and Artaxerxes, his son. I read accounts of the Persians' treaties with neighboring nations, including Israel. I even found a book on the women of ancient Persia.

After reading all those accounts, I had a rich tapestry of information to deepen my novel.

How Contemporary Readers Relate to Historical Characters

How can you make sure a story of the past appeals to people of the present? Simple. Don't major on the historical events, but center the story on your characters and their *unchanging human frailties.* People are people, no matter when they live. They love, they suffer, they go to war, they raise children, they seek meaning and honor in their lives . . . or not. No matter when they lived, some people strive to be good; some people choose to do evil, but each man justifies his actions according to his individual moral code.

Basic human emotional needs do not change. We have them in common with our forefathers, and they are the key to helping your modern reader bond with your historical characters.

Focus on your characters as they strive and grow through difficult tasks, and your contemporary readers will relate because we face the same sorts of challenges. Give your historical characters universal flaws—greed, jealousy, rivalry, lack, bitterness, a desire for revenge, a yearning for love—and set them in their unique time and place.

Don't spend most of your time writing about historical events—write about people moving *through* historical events, resisting change, struggling to survive, striving to protect the ideals and the people they love—and you'll create a gripping story.

I'm often asked if we're "allowed" to use real people in historical novels. Of course! Just be aware that relatively contemporary people have traceable histories, and the more famous that person, the more material already exists on him or her. If you unwittingly get something wrong, you may rouse the ire of historians.

In several of his novels, Caleb Carr has used historical people as peripheral characters. These "real" people add a note of authenticity to his story without forcing him to become an expert on that famous person's history.

Describing the Unfamiliar

The historical novelist shares a problem with fantasy and science fiction writers: how can we avoid stopping the action and yet show our character using or wearing or eating something a modern reader won't immediately understand? If you stop to explain, for instance, what a *trebuchet* is or how it works, an editor is likely to scrawl RUE (resist the urge to explain) in the margin.

So—how do you avoid static paragraphs of explanation? You *show the object at work or in use.* Like this:

> Rulf hoisted the basket of stones to his shoulder and stared at the massive trebuchet making slow progress up the hill. A dozen of

the king's men strained at its side, sweat runneling down their backs as they pushed at the groaning timber frame.

Finally the foreman called a halt. The men braced the wheels and pulled the ropes that lowered the bucket to the platform, then one of them looked up and motioned to Rulf and the others who perspired beneath their heavy loads.

Rulf lumbered forward and scanned the city wall for the glint of bronze-tipped spears. Behind the crenellations, a pair of enemy archers peered through an opening and eyed his progress. With any luck, they wouldn't waste an arrow on him, a mere beast of burden.

Grunting, he tipped his basket into the wooden bucket, then backed away. When loaded with stones and boiling oil, the trebuchet might inflict some damage after the first launch, but he was willing to bet that he'd be climbing this hill many more times before sunset. A wall like that wouldn't crumble easily.

After reading the above paragraphs, you still may not know the dictionary definition of *trebuchet*, but I'll bet you're visualizing one of those medieval machines that flings a bucketful of rocks and/or boiling oil on and over a city wall. That's all you need to know—and active description is much more effective than stopping the story action to insert a dictionary entry.

The same holds true for historical events. Don't halt the action to relate a history lesson, detail a genealogy, or explain backstory. If you've made us care about your characters, don't cheat us of a minute with them.

Underline this: don't write any paragraphs your reader is

going to skim.

In *Stein on Writing*, Sol Stein says: "In fiction, when information obtrudes the experience of the story pauses. Raw information comes across as an interruption, the author filling in. The fiction writer must avoid anything that distracts from the experience even momentarily. A failure to understand this . . . is a major reason for the rejection of novels."[3]

You are There

How can you write a scene that makes your reader feel as if they are standing in the same room as your protagonist? You do it by invoking sensory details. Don't be so caught up in relating dialogue and action that you forget to make your reader's senses tingle. Help him not only see and hear the event of the scene, but smell, taste, touch, and intuit details, too.

Notice the sensory details in this brief bit from my novel about Esther. I've bolded words that evoke something to hear, see, taste, touch, or smell.

As girls, Parysatis and I had often remarked about the discernible difference in the city's atmosphere when the king was away from his palace. We had **groaned** about how boring and dull Susa was without him, but that difference was magnified a hundredfold when one lived in the royal fortress. When I'd entered the palace, the harem **buzzed** with activity and **every slave walked with a brisk** step, never lingering for more than a moment in any one spot. But once the king and his household departed, an air of somnolence descended over the place.

Those of us who had been gathered into the complex reserved for virgins grew sluggish and **lazy in the heat**. We were still fed

> **choice foods** (Artystone claimed the eunuchs were fattening us like lambs for the slaughter) and given our beauty treatments: each morning we bathed in waters **laced with myrrh,** and each evening our handmaids **massaged perfumed** oils into our skin. I had already begun to notice the difference—when I removed my tunic each night, the fabric **smelled of sweet flowers.**

By sprinkling your prose with words that evoke sensory details, you are placing your reader in the scene. Some words and phrases are more loaded than others—for instance, if I write "the sag-bellied rat skittered across the prison's stone floor," you can almost hear the chink of chains, see the damp wetness of the rocks, and smell the odor of filth and disease.

Historical Dialogue

We might as well admit it—people of yesteryear spoke differently than we do today. Not only were their accents unlike ours, but their language was more formal—or less formal, depending upon whether you're writing about cavemen or the founding fathers.

If you insist on writing dialogue that sounds exactly like your characters would speak it, you may lose readers because few people have the patience to sift through dense, boring dialogue. Never forget that we are a video generation. We have grown up with television and movies; we are used to stories that flow past our eyes. Consequentially, we don't have a lot of patience.

Dialogue is not and should not be exact spoken speech. Exact speech is dull, even if you're writing the conversations of twenty-first century Americans. So much of what we say is senseless filler.

"Hey."
"Hey yourself."

"Where ya been?"
"Nowheres."
"Jeet?"
"Had a burger 'n fries."
"Yeah, well. Henry's coming over."

Dull, dull, and hard to read besides. Learn how to condense your character's dialogue so that it includes only important information plus a sprinkling of color.

> Len greeted Chip with the usual greeting,
> then informed him that his dead uncle Henry
> was on his way over.

See? Sometimes you don't need dialogue at all. Or you can introduce it with narrative and *then* let it take off.

Since dialog is not real speech, don't be tempted to write phonetically despite what you've read in *Gone with the Wind*. Writing like this—*luheek thuh suhoond uh doomzdeh*—is too hard to read. (Translation: "like the sound of doomsday" written in an Irish dialect.)

Instead of foisting strange spellings on your reader, indicate a dialect by word choice: "Sure, and don't I know you're goin' with me?" (Still speaking like an Irish woman, but without the impossible spellings.)

A single dropped "g" and appropriate word choice can effectively convey a dialect and not distract your reader from the story.

I enjoy traveling to places where I set my books, and on my trips I always carry a little notebook. In it I jot any unusual (to me) word choices that I might be able to use in a book. For instance, in the United States a sign on a stony hillside would say, "Watch for Falling Rocks." In Ireland, a similar sign said, "Mind Your Windscreen."

At Disney World, as you step off the monorail you hear, "Watch your step." In London, as you step out of the subway you hear "Mind the gap."

In Ireland, I picked up little phrases like these:

I tried to ring him
He was a lovely man
He was all of a dither
He's a lovely little fella
The cheek of him!
He was obviously having me on
He was chancin' his arm.

Having access to little conversation fillers like these can give your dialog loads of color. In the same way, as you read original documents from your chosen historical period, keep a list of phrases you might be able to employ in your dialog. Here are a few from my notes on the Elizabethan period:

I do beg and pray you
Mind your manners, varlet
Hold, sirrah
Mark me
Is aught amiss?
I trow you could
Pray do not tell
Nothing of import
Beshrew this
A pox on him!

In the same vein, be aware of your readers' sensibilities. Profanity is repulsive to many readers, and you can often create the same effect by writing some variation of "He cursed" instead of using profanity. Words that were powerful oaths in Shakespeare's day (Zounds!) don't usually offend most contemporary readers because we're unfamiliar with the word's meaning and connotation (God's wounds—swearing by Christ's wounds). On the other hand, some words that offend today wouldn't have offended a previous generation . . . yet you are writing for contemporary readers.

Historical novelist Stephanie Grace Whitson says, "I do not have my white people calling my black people what white people called black people back then. I do not have my white people thinking about my Lakota people what white people thought about Lakota people back then. And I certainly do not have my people (except the bad ones) *smell* like they smelled back then."[4]

Novels are never completely realistic (and neither is TV. Have you ever wondered when Jack Bauer finds time to go to the restroom?) And no matter how much research we do, we who have been molded by twenty-first century events and culture may never fully understand the mindsets of previous generations. I don't suppose a novelist can ever write a novel that is totally accurate and true to the period. We aim for verisimilitude, we strive to never contradict historical fact, but we must acknowledge that we write for modern readers.

I cringe every time I watch "I Love Lucy" and see Ricky spanking his wife. That TV show, which aired its final episode around the time I was born, presents a mindset in which it's okay for men to strike their wives. Few people flinched in the 1950s; some people probably thought Ricky was being funny. But cultural perspectives change, sometimes drastically.

If you want your novel to reach the emotional core of your present-day reader, you need to keep her perceptions and attitudes in mind so she won't be ripped out of the story you're trying to tell.

Historical fiction pairs story with a rich tapestry of sights, sounds, tastes, aromas, textures, and challenges. Historical novelists strive to be true to their chosen historical period; but they must keep their modern readers in mind—after all, the story is written for them.

When written well, contemporary readers come away feeling that they've not only had a moving emotional experience, but they've lived and learned in a fascinating era far removed from the twenty-first century.

Writing a historical novel may be more involved than

writing a contemporary story, but the rewards and the experience are worth the extra work.

Now . . . what era are *you* eager to write about?

Thank you for purchasing this book in **Writing Lessons from the Front.** If you find any typos in this book, please write and let us know where they are: hunttypos@gmail.com.

We would also appreciate it if you would be kind enough to leave a review of this book on Amazon. Thank you!

ABOUT THE AUTHOR

Angela Hunt writes for readers who have learned to expect the unexpected from this versatile writer. With nearly five million copies of her books sold worldwide, she is the best-selling author of more than 130 works ranging from picture books (*The Tale of Three Trees*) to novels and nonfiction.

Now that her two children have reached their twenties, Angie and her husband live in Florida with Very Big Dogs (a direct result of watching *Turner and Hooch* too many times). This affinity for mastiffs has not been without its rewards—one of their dogs was featured on *Live with Regis and Kelly* as the second-largest canine in America. Their dog received this dubious honor after an all-expenses-paid trip to Manhattan for the dog and the Hunts, complete with VIP air travel and a stretch limo in which they toured New York City. Afterward, the dog gave out pawtographs at the airport.

Angela admits to being fascinated by animals, medicine, unexplained phenomena, and "just about everything." Books, she says, have always shaped her life— in the fifth grade she learned how to flirt from reading *Gone with the Wind*.

Her books have won the coveted Christy Award, several Angel Awards from Excellence in Media, and the Gold and Silver Medallions from *Foreword Magazine*'s Book of the Year Award. In 2007, her novel *The Note* was featured as a Christmas movie on the Hallmark channel. She recently completed her doctorate in biblical literature and is now finishing her doctorate in Theology.

When she's not home writing, Angie often travels to teach writing workshops at schools and writers' conferences. And to talk about her dogs, of course. Readers may visit her web site at www.angelahuntbooks.com.

Selected Novels by Angela Hunt

Passing Strangers
The Offering
The Fine Art of Insincerity
Five Miles South of Peculiar
The Face
Let Darkness Come
The Elevator
The Novelist
The Awakening
The Truth Teller
Unspoken
Uncharted
The Justice
The Canopy
The Immortal
Doesn't She Look Natural ?
She Always Wore Red
She's In a Better Place
The Pearl
The Note
The Debt
Then Comes Marriage
The Shadow Women
Dreamers
Brothers
Journey
Roanoke
Jamestown
Hartford
Rehoboth
Charles Towne
The Proposal
The Silver Sword
The Golden Cross
The Velvet Shadow
The Emerald Isle

ENDNOTES

[1] *The Writer's Digest Character Naming Sourcebook*, by Sherrilyn Kenyon. Cincinnati, OH: Writer's Digest Books, 1994, 2010, 2014.

[2] A free trial copy of Scrivener can be downloaded from www.literatureandlatte.com. Versions for Mac and PC.

[3] Sol Stein, *Stein on Writing*. New York: St. Martin's Press, 1995, p. 7.

[4] Personal correspondence with Stephanie Grace Whitson, 2008.